Waiting for Pairing

Waiting for Pairing

Lauren Megard

Columbus, Ohio

Waiting for Pairing

Published by Gatekeeper Press
2167 Stringtown Rd, Suite 109
Columbus, OH 43123-2989
www.GatekeeperPress.com

ISBN (paperback): 9781662917738

Dedication

To 17-year-old me:

you're making it. One day at a time.

Contents

Acknowledgments

Here's to the 2017 shit that I never dealt with.

In Limbo

I sat there
And waited for them to tell me
That they could get a flicker of life back

Unfortunately, your fire was already burning elsewhere

Our time together suddenly extinguished
And my flame became dull.

We celebrated

We laughed

We exchanged our love

Then this world suddenly protected you no longer.

I feel euphoric
Visited by those I've lost

I'm flying
I'm falling in love again
I have no further expectations from this life

Then I wake up
And find myself longing to live this way once more

I hope you can still see how I've prospered

Please don't forget to check in on me.

I want you to see me
And feel proud of the person I've grown to be.

How naïve I was

In believing I could save everyone

The emotion
Is nowhere to be found inside of me

When I'm living this fast-paced, distraction-filled
life
I'm alone

Then it strikes me
Rapid and sharp
And pools out of me
Like a wound that won't clot.

November 2017

She was concerned about my worrying
"What part of your future do you have to worry about?"

I told her about how I was afraid to fail
And the possibility of running out of options

She disagreed

She told me the worst thing that could happen
Would be if something detrimental took its toll on one of us

We were all together.
We were healthy.
I was supported.

Then, a month later, that worst-case scenario
became a reality right before our eyes

It happened to us.
It happened to her.

I am not a content soul

I look to the past

I daydream about what could be

I'm expected to plant myself in the present, where I confront my greatest enemy:

Realism.

Do you know what it's like?

The need to jump out of your skin
While you're trapped behind bones?

I wake up from a dream
Or hear those blaring sirens

I pick up the phone to call you
Caution will forever be an apparent feeling

Just tell me you are okay
So I know I'm not losing another for an extra day

Some stages are more mundane than others
Nonetheless, we are always reminded of the
inevitable
I heard you, and I'm coming.

I love you

But who am I without you?

–Symptom of co-dependence

Sometimes I choose to live in the past

Because that's where she is

–Trouble turning the page

I remember learning to sit with myself

How uncomfortable it is to be present without interruption
How difficult it is to reflect in a world full of distractions

Instead of feeling the pain
We reach for an ounce of dopamine

We leave our emotions on shelves
Fearing we carry too much baggage

We must dust them off and feel them to their full extent despite this fear

It isn't until we reopen these feelings that we come to realize that the wearying part of our journey has been conquered

I'm sitting in the back of a moving car
I look to the front
but there is no driver

I crawl forward
but my attempt to gain control is unattainable
I find myself trapped

Then it always ends the same

I scream as I find the car progressing closer to my catastrophic peril…
…Darkness

–Reoccurring Nightmares

Time doesn't heal all

Instead of smothering the memories, it hangs a white transparent curtain between you and the affliction

My heart melted that day
Over time, it hardened into cement

I'm left with skin, bones, and the heavy bitterness I carry in my chest

I have an addiction
To seeing a different reality

I'm sinking into a daydream
A world I wrote myself
Although there is a pre-existing universe

Feet on the ground
Focus. Focus. Focus.

It erupted in seconds
Everything a blur
My brain full of fire

Hours go by and the damage is done

I'm left to pick up the pieces and clean the debris
within my smoke-filled mind

I'm exhausted

And I need somewhere to rebegin

I always told myself
That if the circumstances had been different
I would have pursued the future I always wanted

But I realized it wasn't my environment stopping
me

It was me.

I wondered why the earth kept spinning
When my world stopped in its tracks
I wanted it all to come to a standstill
Just as I had.

I'm significant,

I assured myself in that fleeting glimpse of time.

It never could have been any different
Because it already happened the way it did

No amount of wondering or guilt
Will ever change the outcome

Now repeat that in your head over and over again

Try to make the feelings of regret and knowledge of
the butterfly effect subside

I do not need advice or a solution
I just need to be acknowledged
As I carry the weight of it all

I dropped into the unknown
Forced to find meaning
Through what they call 'soul-searching'

I kept trudging
Inhaling anguish along the way

They asked if we wanted to keep a lock of your hair
Dad requested the piece to be a big one

I was home alone,
My eyes on the envelope that contained your lock of hair.
I lifted it out
And gripped the last remaining piece of you
Sobbing as I looked at your photo on the mantel

I'm sorry,
I said.

I'm so sorry.

After all these years

Attempting to heal

This is how it manifests

Into beta-blockers

Anti-depressants

Whatever helps me sleep

Whatever suppresses the feelings that nauseate me.

They stop asking how you're doing

Instead, they ask you
Why you haven't moved on.

Because time heals everything.
Right?

I miss the version of me
That existed when you were around

My identity vanished
My world altered
Who am I supposed to be without you?

One thing I knew I wasn't
Was a child
No longer

Isolation is my friend
It comforts me to know that I won't feel as though
I'm floating

I'm grounded but guilty
As weeks become months
And my mind becomes loud
From thoughts unspoken

They say that, after the initial blow,
It's best to prevent any substantial life changes to
make room to heal

But I was only seventeen
And when you're seventeen, it's important to look
to your future

Decide what your career will look like
Digest the rest later

Grief of any kind

Is a question even you can't answer

Never forget
What evolution has granted us

Underneath the thread
Is functionality within the factory

Until it serves its purpose
And our establishment returns to dust

I see pieces of you
Wherever I go
While happy memories embed in those fragments
of time

They will never assemble into a present form
They will never assemble into a visual you

You can cry

You can scream

You can acknowledge that it hurts

You can learn to carry the unfixable

These hands on the steering wheel
Don't feel like mine
I'm controlling a character
That has come forward
In this two-dimensional universe

I know your body feels as heavy as a boulder
And your mind is overwhelmed with heartbreak
and unspoken words

But as soon as you force yourself to take your first
impenetrable step,
The weight slowly becomes less and less dominant
with each foot you tread

To complete the conclusion of your story
You must come to terms with the beginning of it
And forgive the circumstances of the past

Hardship showed me
Those who said they loved me
Those who said they cared about me
Those who said they would support me

Until the blunt reality washed away those empty words
Leaving the minority behind

Those who showed they loved me
Those who showed they cared deeply for me
Those who supported me through the thick of it all

I felt so safe when I was younger
Surrounded by those who were so sure of every
circumstance

As I grew older, I realized that stability had
vanished
As I never had an idea of what I was meant to do

But little did I know
That neither did they

Finding strength in humility
In being confused
In questioning your knowledge and spirituality
In asking for help
Is not a weakness
But one of the greatest human superpowers you
find within yourself

She once told me:
"Someday, you'll find yourself filled with such an abundance of joy that you'll feel you could explode."

Ever since, I wondered when the heavy emotions keeping me at rock bottom would fizzle out

And the feelings would rise high
Bursting out of the ditch I'd sat in that day

I despise my brain
For malfunctioning
When placed in a world
That expects our minds to be nothing less
Than high functioning
In an almost robotic manner

Sometimes the feeling of growth
Can bring a sense of gloom
For I will never be as happily ignorant
As I used to be

I was too busy sacrificing everything
For the things I wanted
That my vision became skewed

When I had awakened,
I realized I'd sacrificed the things I'd needed
The vital things that I already had

Grief can be found in the most bittersweet corners
of life
Celebration and happy memories
Never exclude bouts of heartbreak
Even in life's most nostalgic places

Some days feel as though
An anchor has been tied to my ankle
And I begin to sink in the exact spot I no longer
stand in

I'm planted at the bottom with the weight of it all
Stuck with no chance of rising above

I want nothing more

Than to watch the mask I feel I must wear

Burn to ashes

So that I'm forced to face the fear

Of the possibility of others being aloof

After my memories and authenticity

Come forward

Please don't tell me

That my time is up

Before I can escape the bars in front of my own mind

I tell myself

All of those wasted seconds

Will be reclaimed, somehow

They're all so sure
That they have the right answers for you

As though your path belongs to them

They choose to doubt you and tell you to use your head
Until you become successful somewhere else
And they long for a piece of your prosperity

The most sorrowful feeling
Comes from parting with those you love
Stay safe. Okay?

The greatest gift that this earth could never provide me
Is a place that you would come home to once again.

The days in between
The excitement and distractions
Can be the most tranquil or dismal days

I am relaxed or forced to face the things I have
deeply packed away

My present residence
No longer feels like home

It belongs in old tapes and family films
For those tapes never change over time
The way I have

If letting go of the things that no longer serve me is so helpful,
Then why are they the hardest to let go?

The days begin to blur
Like watercolor on paper
Revealing an abstract piece
Full of beauty and vibrance
Or a blotchy nightmare

I'm still searching for the light at the end of the tunnel
That I just can't seem to find

I wish you were here to tell me what it's like
To know all the answers
To be showered with closure

If you could stand in front of me for one day
The inner child I used to be
I'd take you to all the places that birthed your most loved memories
Walking down the sidewalk of the Chicago suburbs
Before fuel was added to the fire

Small storm cloud
Drifting in the back of my mind
You follow me everywhere
Almost concealed deep in my head

I suddenly wonder
Why the feelings you accompany
Must reside in my thoughts
Like an intrusive guest
That refuses to depart

I feel unreliable
As the simplest things seem to drain
My stamina
My concentration
My energy

I feel like the excuses are running out
For the only true defense is one hard to admit
And the only one that would shatter my ego

We grow up
And realize what we're worth

Allowing those around us
To walk over us
Is now realized as a weakness
A boundary that mustn't be crossed

It's hard to depict
Whether my dreamlike state
Was truly a dream
Or a harsh reality

I don't want to let go of this moment
For I know it will be one of the memories I will
mourn
And attempt to run back to in my head
Comparing the light to my lonely state

And I will never be the same

As of now, I'm watching life from my windowpane

Attempting to learn

Who this changed soul became

I see your bittersweet resemblance in me
The sound of our laughs
The same crooked smile
The identical birthmark
I carry pieces of you on my skin and in my mind

I'd rather people feel comfortable to speak to me
About the difficult things
Than to never bring it to my attention at all

It reminds me that you and our bank of memories
Will never be forgotten

Oh, how my sunny disposition
Can turn into quite a sour one

I wonder, when I wake up,
Which will overpower the other

Why couldn't I hold on

When the storm came?

It swept me up and I lost one of the most

important things I knew:

Control

The most daunting thing I could've ever lost

Looking at the screen,
We see people we should be like

In the city
On the rooftops
Walking across a sandy beach

If only I could have that

Comparison and expectations
Of things that aren't truly real
Will be the death of my mind

Everyone wants to have a story to tell
An opinion based on said experience

To be hilarious, wise and different
Seems so difficult when everyone competes for the for the same recognition

I hope that someday,
I can look back at my younger self
Mistakes made, lessons learned, the terrifying things
she had to face
And feel relieved that she never gave up

Over time,

Fresh memories begin to chip

Like paint on a cement classroom wall,

Pieces begin to diminish

As do moments of the past

With joy and relief,

You watched me enter this world

With terror and sadness,

I watched you leave it

Some days, I manage to find a small corner of
peace
I attempt to hold onto these spaces

Although I know nothing lasts forever,
I will find my way to this place once again

I want to keep going
Knowing that I have not yet met every soul I will grow to love in this lifetime
Including mine

Being able to get out of my own head and live
Is the most important yet difficult advice I've ever received
As the healthy habits following this advice
Are challenging actions to perform

The simplest things we take for granted
Are the things that others forever fight to achieve

When I close my eyes,
I'm unable to stay exactly where my body lies

I find myself falling

Down, down, down

We will be endlessly different

Our edge has dulled

But we continue to wake

And mold our outlines into something beautiful

Something bigger than ourselves

So much time

Work

Dedication

For things that will cease to exist someday

To the people around us, losses may seem as
though they've taken place so long ago
When it's a daily cycle we continue to work around

If only we could run

From all the noise

Far away from everything that is grey

I feel as though the storm
Quickly washed away my youth
And left me battered in the aftermath

So I'll walk toward the sunshine with my healing scars
Just as she would have wanted me to

They told me you were bright, colorful and bold
Just as you were in life

I had no choice in where I currently am
With the world finding ways to sway my reality

But I have the choice in changing my ending

Oh, how history repeats itself

Telling us the same story each and every time

As we expect things to change

When the same mistakes are made

I'm exhausted from the lies
My brain chooses to tell me
That the worst-case scenario
Is always upon me

And if he

Had listened to my bargain

To switch places with you

I would've

If you're currently hoping for it to be painless
It'll find its way in

Being avoidant and pushing it away
Hoping for a great escape
Will only make the agony force itself in sharper

Some days,

I continuously kick the small pebble laying in my path

Others, I struggle to propel the boulder forward

3 minutes

We're on our way

2 minutes

Our world and everything in it shatters

1 minute

Everything moves on without us

Would I rather

Count on the amount of time I believe I still have

Or do the living now, when I know I may die

young?

I hope wherever I land
I'll hold the promise we all kept

I'll come and find you
Just don't forget about me in the meantime

These cards you've been dealt
You either play them or quit the game

The only thing that decides how lucky you are
After your initial draw
Are your conditions

Things that are easier said than done:
Let go of looking back
Learn to live again

Love Letters of all Kinds

When you were in her presence,
You were home

She had no choice but to vacate,
And we became nomads
As we knew we would never reside in a home just
as wonderful.

If we had known the circumstances,
We would still run back to you
Every time

Thank you for allowing me

To find a home in you

Placing different yet lovely things on our table

Year after year

"You have such an excitement for life

And I hope you never lose that."

–Mom, 2003

And we all found solace in each other
From youth to young adult,
We made crazy promises
Only friends could keep

Although I'll have come and gone,

Your favorite song will forever play in my head

Swimming in our visions
Feeling the sun on our skin

No one has ever made me laugh
Or forget everything else but that moment
Quite like you have

We watched as all these thoughts rushed around
our heads as we grew older
But we never stopped laughing
Like the little kids we were

Thank you for being the only friends I ever needed

I haven’t met you,
But maybe you’ll be one of the souls
I grow to love someday

Candy-eyed

Lying next to you

Nothing can hurt us now

Until we move on,

I'll remember our carefree and unstoppable

moments

I know how hard on yourself you are
Thinking it's taboo to speak highly of yourself

Let the thought enter and pass
For you deserve so much more from yourself

Note to Self

It's okay
To be closed off
From sharing certain aspects of your life
With other people

You're allowed to let it be yours

"Do you know how to eat an elephant?

One piece at a time?"

–Silly yet crucial advice from Dad

Many say

You must be surrounded by those you love

To heal

However

There is no shame in feeling lonely

Or choosing to heal certain parts of yourself alone

You don't have to allow anyone to tell you how to manage your wellbeing
Without permission
Your health is not for outsiders to analyze

Treat yourself with gentleness

No matter what version of yourself you wake up as

I know you want to slow things down
As the days constantly run a marathon in your head

It's hard to come to a standstill
You must find some comfort in the chaos

No one has the power to give me back what is already mine

My visions may not be visible to those around me
But they are still so very clear inside my mind

The secular world is unable to leave crowded
thoughts at bay
Don't push them away
You will see clearly soon enough

Things can stand unresolved

Don’t let them keep you from feeling hopeful

Sitting in silence
Will only continue to strain your relationship

With difficult things unsaid
Comes a mound of misunderstanding

When you see someone deplore over something
trite
Hold your bitterness
And find empathy in knowing that it is the worst
pain they have ever felt

Ignorance is bliss

You are so observant
And feel so deeply

Find what you need
To re-energize

Question your spirituality
Question the human condition
Question why you feel the way you do

The universe may teach you something about yourself

I cling to scenarios that I know may never happen
But what if I'm exactly where I'm supposed to be?

The future I dream of will come
In time

And so, the pages will keep turning without you
And I will continue to carry the pieces of you
As I sculpt the fine details of who I am and who I strive to be

I hope that, every so often,
You still choose to look back and wave
With your beautiful, crooked smile
With a look of joy in your eyes

Knowing you have given me every single tool
In our short and life-changing time together

I hope you're doing well
And have found a safe journey home

I love you.

The End
(For Now)

About the Author

Lauren Megard is a social work student at UWRF. She currently lives in a dinky apartment in her college town but hopes to further explore the world because cornfields get extremely tiring to look at. Lauren is absolutely terrible at math but feels at home when reading or writing – particularly when writing to create closure in things that can't be simply answered.

www.ingramcontent.com/pod-product-compliance
Lightning Source LLC
Chambersburg PA
CBHW051808050726
47598CB00006B/2468

* 9 7 8 1 6 6 2 9 1 7 7 3 8 *